TENDER TAXES

Tender Taxes

Versions of Rilke's French Poems

JO SHAPCOTT

To Fiara

best

Jo Shapcott

October 2001

ff

faber and faber

First published in 2001
by Faber and Faber Limited
3 Queen Square London WC1N 3AU
Published in the United States by Faber and Faber, Inc.,
an affiliate of Farrar, Straus and Giroux LLC, New York

Typeset by Faber and Faber Limited
Printed in Italy

A CIP record for this book
is available from the British Library

ISBN 0-571-20252-7

2 4 6 8 10 9 7 5 3 1

Contents

THE ROSES

TENDER TAXES

Foreword

In 1991 I first opened my copy of Rilke's French poems in A. Poulin Jr's Graywolf Press edition. I already knew and loved his German poems and was surprised to find he had written nearly four hundred in French as well, most of them in the last four years before his death in 1926. I knew almost at once that I wanted to write something in response to the French poems, but what transpired was not translation: my poems became instead responses, arguments, even dramatisations. I've called them 'versions' here, reluctantly. We don't yet have the word for this kind of exchange.

The first ten poems in Rilke's sequence *Les Fenêtres* were originally published the year after his death in an edition with illustrations by his lover Balandine Klossowska, or 'Merline' as she was also known. The engravings throw fresh light on the poems; the whole project seems redolent with private meaning for them both. Windows had a special significance for them, we know, the subject of their conversations as well as writing and drawing. In a letter to Merline in 1920 Rilke says of a sketch she sent him: 'The Girl at the Window (if ony I could believe it mine!), one of those windows we talked about in Fribourg, no a hundred, a thousand windows in one – a tragic frame to this gesture which, in raising up her hair, seems to form the image of a cry, Arm, oh arm!'

In *Les Fenêtres*, the speaker sometimes addresses the windows of the title and sometimes an absent woman. The diction is always is formal. Poulin translates a line from poem IV as 'You, window, O waiting's measure', for example. My challenge was to make this kind of utterance sound natural, contemporary. I had to invent a modern voice to speak the poems, the voice of someone you could imagine spending a good deal of time alone in a room and capable of speaking aloud to windows and a woman who is never there. The result (to my mind anyway) is a cross between Chandler's Philip Marlowe and Rilke, though I suspect the poems still harbour more Rilkean intensity than this description might suggest.

The collection of Rilke's French poems that was published in Paris in 1926 included a sequence of poems called *The Valaisian Quatrains*. These celebrate the landscape of the Valais in Switzerland, where he found a refuge to write in the last years of his life. In a group of poems which owe so much to the pastoral tradition it's surprising to find so few intimations of death, or danger, or of the city in the distance. Rilke's sense of the pastoral is wholly idyllic, containing only beauty, fulfilment and transcendence. Even the peasants are solid, happy and fruitful. His letters of that time paint a darker picture of the place and of his mood but his poems suppress any blot on the landscape, almost as if he's found a way to use sheer description as a means to draw closer to God.

My version of pastoral is uneasy. I moved Rilke's poems, set them in a place which has, literally, an edgier feel: the borders of Wales, where my family has its roots. In my poems the place names change from Swiss to Welsh and English.

A sequence of tiny poems called *Les Roses* was also published in Rilke's collection *Vergers* in 1926. Many of his German poems, including 'The Rose Window', dwell on roses, too, and they surface again and again in his letters to Merline. He wrote, excitedly, for example, how a 'little bunch of roses arrived only yesterday, Monday morning. It belonged to me in its every significance.'

I began to see that in the sequence Rilke's roses were women. And more than that – petal – space – petal – these poems were versions of female genitalia. Once this perception had taken hold I knew I couldn't follow Rilke's pattern of addressing the roses: he speaks to them, tells them what they are like, what makes them up, where their essence is to be found. My roses are given their own voice. They speak. And if you put my poems alongside Rilke's, more often than not you'll find my roses addressing his, saying, in effect: 'It's not like that, it's like this.' And, for me, this parachuted the whole notion of gender relations into the business of translation. Who's doing what to whom? And, more importantly, how does a woman poet relate to the poets who have gone before? Finally, though, just as I believe Rilke's roses to be one extended love poem, so mine became the same and, in the end, a love poem to him.

My engagement with the French Rilke took place over ten years. Looking back, I can see that this is primarily a reader's book: a record of the way an author who was important to me moved into my house and, during all those imaginary discussions readers have with writers, became as close as a profound friend, or an intimate enemy, or a lover. The result was unexpected – not a collection of translations but this tender and taxing conversation.

Jo Shapcott
2001

Acknowledgements

Thanks are due to the editors of *Poetry London Newsletter* and *PN Review*, where early versions of some of these poems appeared, and to the BBC's *Poetry Proms* for commissioning six of the 'Gladestry Quatrains'. 'The Windows' and 'The Roses' were first published in *Phrase Book* and *My Life Asleep* respectively. Warm thanks to Northern Arts and the University of Newcastle for their support during the writing of this book. The quotations from Rilke's letters in the Foreword are from *Letters to Merline*, translated by Jesse Brown (London: Robson Books, 1990). I am indebted to A. Poulin Jr's edition of *The Complete French Poems of Rainer Maria Rilke* (St Paul: Graywolf Press, 1979), which introduced me to these poems.

The First Lie

I'm the little toy you'll shatter,
the garden with miraculous
hiding places. You dart in and out
just to be half-found.

I'm the wind that sings in Braille,
your own shadow getting longer,
the beautiful holes that whimper
in your brain.

THE WINDOWS

10 a.m.

It's enough that all the things
around are more real than anything else,
more real than me. The furniture, balcony,
doors, the windows, I spoke to them
and they talked back.

Then a woman, shy, came into the picture
and the windows flattened back into the walls,
the furniture sat down again on the carpet.
Her arms, hair, smell made the dead things
quiet again. I knew I would lose her too.

11 p.m.

I won't stop talking to you just because
you're acting strange. You mouthed off
all day yesterday, blinds flapping in the breeze
and now, not a peep out of you, and
the thin curtain only just moving.

I'm waiting, listening, could wait all day;
it doesn't diminish me to look a fool
with my cheek against the glass for hours.
I've got time and time and a triumphant soul
because you'll crack eventually
and let me through or let me in.

Noon

Talking to you like this
makes everything clear.
The lines that shape the world
glow so I understand them.

A woman may be beautiful
but I can tolerate even that
when you put yourself
between us, making us look.

No chance that who I am
can get lost in this space,
small, airy, like love
with me in the middle.

1 p.m.

Is it her dream or mine?
When I invite her home now
she sits near you, leaning.
Forearms, breasts, shoulders.

It's true she's beautiful
and knows how to place
herself just so, especially
her long hands on the glass,

the rest of her tense as if
she wanted to jump right through.
She's not enough, although
I might think so if she did go.

2 p.m.

It's true, I do talk to you more
when I'm drunk, the chair pulled up close,
my forehead and the glass in my hand
pressed against the pane.

My nose is so
close up I can see
the separate pores
reflected on your surface.

So there's me, or my face at least,
but all the time the shadow
of something else, the dirt
on the glass, the big mess outside.

3 a.m.

I'm starting to count you now
as though you might hide with the others
around the room if I once
lost track of the numbers.

Did I sit on the sill, or was it
someone I knew, spending hours there,
so it seemed, trying to touch
the one I didn't love with meaning?

I'm drunk again, you know,
so drunk it all gets clearer
for a second, until I glimpse my reflection,
bent double, falling down blind.

4 a.m.

I do want love deep down, somewhere in the back
of my spine.
I watch the window now as if she were a woman
stretching the stars
into dawn, everything a lover must know.
She's mean,
early on, but I like that: it gets me ready
for the sun's explosion
when my eyes don't know what to do
with all that
after the different abandon of the night.

Maybe there's nothing there after all
but the air
though I'm sure the sky must be made of more,
the way the birds
seem to hold on to it, the way they move
their feathers,
the way they measure it, taste it, fuck it
as they fly.

5 a.m.

I feel as if you've made me up.
Here is time, framed,
wearing a jacket that's too big,
draped like a child.

Once I leaned and stayed so long
I looked different: more of a kid
with fewer lines, but it was dawn outside
and the sun drained the detail from the glass.

I think I want you to save me
from love but then it arrives too,
in the wrong mood, beating
against my forehead with wings.

6 a.m.

O boo hoo, O shame.
Window, your skin's wet inside
from my tears and wet
outside with rain.

We've come this close
too late, too soon.
Now I'm dressed up in curtains:
voile, organdie, void.

7 p.m.

Woman, yes, I'm talking
to you now, and I'm watching
you lean out of that window
so far you make me nervous.

You're a poser.
With your beautiful arms up
and your head turned
you give yourself away.

I don't understand gestures
in the dark, the way you use
the window as a backdrop
and me as the blind audience.

8 p.m.

I can't help it, I taste
whatever you have to offer.
You taste of night and day.
You taste of all the weathers.

Maybe that's everything, maybe
nothing, all show for the eyes
keeping me awake in case
I miss something wonderful.

Promises, promises; and all the while
the world shrivels in front of me.
I'm tired and still my eyes gobble roses,
rain forests, oceans, satellites, the moon.

9 a.m.

I'm in the mood for gardening.
I look carefully for the subtle lichens
spreading tiny hairs on the architrave
and even where the glass meets the frame.

Small insects, aeroplanes brush past
our field of vision, birds do, and clouds.
I study each flight path across
the small square, study hard and memorise.

I'm soothed by what's out there, the force
of it. I can watch all day, you know I can,
close as a breath to you but never touching.
Why? To see how to get out.

10 a.m.

Now she's looking hard, watching hard.
The microscope stance by the window. I'm
embarrassed to see her concentrate this much
as though it could help her soul meet the world.

I daren't even glance at her now because I think
I would see right through her eyes to the coils
of her brain. A better man might say her look
watered a garden of images, but it's just not true.

You see, her heart, her heart's just not in it –
too busy counting the number of beats spent
and setting the total against what's left
so we can calculate her name when she's gone.

11 a.m.

I'm a sod in the morning and so are you, sky,
up there, all square, mouthing things at me
and licking the room till it's worn out,
till it sticks out its tongue at you, in return:
two great liars wagging their tongues at each other –
then at me. And watch what you say about me,
or I'll beat you up, I'll beat all the bad tongues;
you say it again and again, you keep talking
about the fall, the rug, the dirty drop into bed.

Midnight

I'm just playing around, window,
fooling my own eyes and you
when I want so much to translate
us both into the sky.

You've pulled out of me a final form
which comes through you, or from you.
There's a crack in the corner
where the putty is loose.

I want to climb and see you
climb too into a new constellation.
You, window, and you, stars, and me,
I want us all to be rhymes.

The Second Lie

Am I flower, am I grass blade?
Am I almost, but not quite, a word?
A new island made of hush,
off the map? One thing's sure:

I'm late for my own creation –
on the eighth day – your afterthought.
You made me and now you must watch
God eat me up bit by bit.

GLADESTRY QUATRAINS

Gwaithla Brook

I'm always cladding myself
in what's just undressed me;
my body's a laugh,
every cell a round, rude wavelet.

So I change my outfit,
even my long hair, my skin.
Behind this kind of flight
my life ripples, totally see-through.

Radnorshire

You'd be arrested – stopped
halfway between earth and sky,
caught drunk in charge,
on voices of water, bronze, beer,

wrong-footed on a slick of oil –
if you didn't warm your hands
on this border country, touch
its crust, finished, like bread.

Hanter Hill

Tiny rose of light
    a wall crumbling in on itself
the slopes of the hill   or of my cheek
       hesitate

while the excess of light
    stamps its feet
in the lane   all over me
     insisting on the wrong route.

Huntington Castle

Borders have castles which
have forgotten whatever passion
drove them to rise, though this one
glances at me with the old look.

Ivy forces into bluestone turrets
which a terrible sun makes gold
when it's not glinting behind arrow-slits
through which the verbals peer.

Gwaithla Road

It's absent-minded, full
of sheep and mud, this lane,
and beautiful light goldsmiths
would want to set into stone.

The rowan in its exact place,
opposes a vertical
against the slow, robust field
which stretches itself and yawns.

Cefn Hir

Do you see, up there, those high pastures of angels,
    among the heather?
In the strange light
    they seem more than far.

Down the clear valley and right up to the ridge
    you can see yourself break
into fragments which float in the air: bird, mite,
    balloon, bat, RAF Hawk.

Dolyhir

Summer Sunday: church bells
        too far away to hear.
When you're working outside the heat
        smells of asphalt and hops.

Strange torpor.
        Racing down the culvert,
though, alert water.
        There is nothing frank about this landscape.

Glascwm

This slope has wings, as do our bats,
    and the dragonflies and every bird,
        flaunting as if resting on updrafts
    could make a creature invisible.

Look, the light doesn't lie heavy on us
    at all, we can move our legs and arms
        through the honey   and even the grass
    wears its worms with grace.

To Muzot from Gladestry

You are the altar where I've brought
these fruits: blackberries, rosehips,
damsons, all the hedgerow berries,
offered up to supplant your words.

Stepping into the field,
I glimpse your wide-brimmed hat
as you pace the vineyard,
looking for the same blessing.

And Back

So I must bring even my flaws,
everything I know to this place.
Wanderer, incomer, borderer,
liar, mother of everything I see.

It's just a garden shed with a desk,
computer and phone line
                        granite step
window on an oak, wires and music.

Song in the Shed

Today it's a profane tower,
I warm myself on the old heater
to ripen: the work will be sweet,
the work will be good, I murmur.

In here, every day is Sunday,
the amount of prayer going on —
to make it good, to make it sweet –
like the music from a carillon.

When it's sweet, when it's good
it's more Saturday night down the Oak
where the jokes fall drop by drop
into the crowd, fall upwards, for luck.

Newchurch

The year
    turns
        on the talk
of weather.

Humid air,
    the rains,
        blankets
of mists, a bluster

of words
    for each
        day's
condition.

Even graveyards
    here collapse, catch
        fire, give up
on their dead.

Old Radnor

Mauve rose in the high grass,
hedges in straight lines,
the sky looking down
scornfully, and at me.

I'm sad, in that incomer way,
ardent and small. I don't understand
why the same past is different for us,
why I remember and the sky forgets.

Colva

How old is the grass I'm standing on?
Or the earth where it's rooted?
Younger than my computer icons
for e-mail, sky, wind, trash and bread.

Yesterday's still propagating
in my body cells, in my synapses
and on the contours of this land underfoot
which consents much more easily to it.

Lower Gwaithla

The night the comet met the lunar eclipse
calm penetrated us from the sky;
my palm blocked whole constellations
when I held up my hand to the Milky Way.

The little waterfall just below
sang to drown out my breath:
still fast and shallow,
still drunk on space.

Caety Traylow

Before you can count to ten
everything changes: the wind flicks
clarity out of even
the high thistle stalks

and flings it in my face,
so close it can't be seen.
    A precipice
on a border mountain

gives more certain footing
    than this spot where
        long grass displaces itself
overnight,   in wind, in rain,

lies down under the clear air
as if stroked
    by the hand
which made it up.

From Gladestry to Muzot

I'm in a lane that turns and plays
along the escarpment
like a ribbon you might knot
around a summer hat.

You're in a Muzot vineyard, hat
on head as if you'd invented wine.
And what wine: a comet
promised for next year.

Burl Hill

In winter, serious black clouds
make the hill look older, more
its true age, older than the fields,
as old as my most secret body cells.

This mountain's strictly a female deity:
she wants cirrus for the curl of hair
tumbling across her face
with all the other youth of the sky.

Rilke Spotted above Gilwern

Honeysuckle launches out of a hedge
tangled with bindweed, flowers
alert, tongues hanging out
for the moment to close.

You're walking up the lane towards me
with a bouquet of red berries from the hedgerow.
Already? Is summer over? Another step
closer and you'll have autumn for a lover.

Hergest

After a day
of wind
it's suddenly still
and

on the horizon,
    rising up in red terraces
enlightened   gold
        a bas-relief of verbs.

Road Not Available

You know how a man speaking about his mother
suddenly looks like her, mid-sentence, right there?
The fields above the stream often take to gurning
their parents like that, endless remembering

in which they drink their pasts further and further
down, while the hill looks over its shoulder
and seems to start back into pure space, returning
like the pasture to the astonishment of its origin.

Gilwern Lane

Sometimes I hum while working,
and I think the hedge does too:
hawthorn, gap, dog rose, fence.
Of course, we know about the loud stream

making the rest seem quiet
though its song is just the hush
between words which,
in rhythm, advance.

Over the Col

The wind speaks to the land like a linguist
who's known its old words for ages.
She finds the contours hot to touch
but understands just how to say them.

She's unstoppable. In a burst
of élan she's likely to force
out of me an enormous step
backwards, to put me in my place.

Wye Marches

It keeps evading me, this border country,
though my own grandfathers
mined coal, coughed, spat
and died not far away.

You round a corner and the hill
has moved, the sky's gone AWOL
and the ancestors, muttering in another tongue
have dug themselves even further in.

Gilwern Dingle

A lane between two meadows,
not leading anywhere
but still managing to tempt
the fields to go along with it.

A track which often has
nothing   ahead
except the ford,
and the lengthening season.

Llan

If there's a goddess of this place
does she speak Welsh?
There's not much English
in her bright face.

Old border tongues trash
this cwm, words and sounds
I can make when my parents,
rarely, let me eat their ashes.

The valley loves, it sleeps.
Why should I enter its body,
travel its capillaries,
listen to its skin?

Gwaithla Garden

It's like you to spot
the small butterfly near the ground
showing off the illustrations
in its flying manual

and to describe it like that, and the other one
closing in on the edge of the flower
we're all breathing now because
you wrote it in 1922 and, O

beloved, this is not the moment to read you
into it, but to see the fragile blues
scattered, floating and flying
like the blue upstrokes and downstrokes

of this torn-up love letter in the wind
I've been writing you for ages
while the postman
hovered for it at the door.

Mountain Ash

The midges are drawing blood
already, out early tonight.
They're full up – on me – round and wise
like the children of a walnut.

I'm complaining as loudly as the rowan,
which is so cankered it must surely feel pain
though you could imagine the spaces between
the leaves contain enough blue for healing.

Down the track there's movement,
a head bobbing through the greenery:
my daughter wearing her red baseball cap,
a dot offered to the tip of every I.

The Third Lie

I haven't explained myself.
You close your eyes, you leap.
It's almost a devout thing to do,
so God says. Or another trap.

Opening your eyes later
you get remorse like a joke.
Stood next to such a gorgeous lie
you're in danger of looking fake.

THE ROSES

Rosa gallica

If sometimes you're surprised
by my coolness
it's because inside myself,
petal against petal, I'm asleep.

I've been completely awake while my heart
dozed, for who knows how long,
speaking aphids and bees to you in silence,
speaking English through a French mouth.

Rosa hemisphaerica

You see me as half-open,
a book whose pages
can be turned by the wind
then read with your eyes closed;

butterflies stream out,
stunned to discover
they think just like you,
dab wings all over your face.

Rosa foetida

I'm an imperfect thing:
neat, layered
but spilling petals and pollen,
dropping bruised scent

on to the ground.
Essence of roses is not sweet,
but brown at the edges
like the air you breathe.

Rosa centifolia

So you think you caused
the bud to bloom,
enchanted the petals
into smiling.

We're talking Rosa centifolia,
the hundred-petalled rose;
ask the bee, who can't concentrate
on anything else.

Rosa nitida

Space folds against space,
petal touches petal;
you look at me
as though you want to fall in,

make the flower
glow with your own image,
change my meaning
from rose to Narcissus.

Rosa arvenis

One rose is every rose,
so you say, just as one word
might be any other:
sepal, stigma, filament.

But then we can't speak floriculture,
Can't discuss botany at all,
not even mention plant entropy
or the taxonomy of roses.

Rosa pimpinellifolia

O I'm leaning
against your forehead,
against your eyelid,
scenting your skin

with my own,
making you think
you can sleep
inside my face.

Rosa glauca

In my dream I could perform
water acrobatics
and swam with a troupe:
we leaned inwards

to form a perfect rose
which was, I swear,
a dead-ringer for the pattern
in your left iris.

Rosa sancta

Now you've made
a saint out of me,
Saint Rose, open-handed,
she who smells of God naked.

But, for myself, I've learned
to love the whiff of mildew
because though not Eve, exactly,
yes, I stink of the Fall.

Rosa sempervirens

I've only a few hours
of openness; so little time
to exude caresses,
float them in the air.

If you forget what was,
this scent that drenched you,
I'll die but be forced back
to work on miracles.

Rosa damascena

You're inclined to confuse
me with yourself
as if you'd found
a mirror to worship.

I'm guilty too,
breathing you in
to catch a trace
of twice-blooming damask.

Rosa canina

Look, I'm growing
out of your left eye, snagging
your retina with little thorns,
rooting behind your frontal lobes.

What can you see
through the hundred pink tongues,
now you've a pupil who speaks
perfume, attracts bees?

Rosa elegantula

You ask if I'm best friends
with the present, or whether
it's memory I nestle up to.
All the while you fill your mind

with pictures of me: happy,
thirsty, my petals as shrouds,
as potpourri on the bathroom shelf.
You try to read me aloud when you're alone.

Rosa mutabilis

I have vanished.
The table, set for food,
wine glasses, the odd
petal among this stuff.

I know a gesture
for every vase.
I'm the same phrase
only now not sung.

Rosa moschata

I'm cooking up perfume –
attar of roses,
absolute rose –
dancing round the stove.

When you say yes
to smells
everything else
fades in the breeze.

Except eyes,
the music
and, in the middle,
me, dancing.

Rosa foliolosa

You touch me with everything
that's touched you.
Pages and pages
of past butterflies stroke me,

moaning like the dictionary
under the weight of it all
and I tremble, stupid Hybrid Perpetual,
as I let you read me better.

Rosa stellata

Perhaps we share
the same subtle matter
now I've stroked roots
under your skin.

It isn't work, you know,
this opening and closing.
But I can distract even God
into choosing your house.

Rosa odorata

I can't turn a smell
into a single word;
you've no right
to ask. Warmth
coaxes rose fragrance
from the underside of petals.

The oils meet air:
rhodinol is old rose;
geraniol, like geranium;
nerol is my essence
of magnolia; eugenol,
a touch of cloves.

Rosa pteracantha

Spinning in the wind
so fast even the thrips,
my little petal-scarring insects,
fly off dizzy, so fast

you can't touch me
without risking a thorn,
can only watch as my heart
is shaken out into the world.

Rosa Mundi

O God, here I stand,
feet in my own grave,
smiling, lifting your face
in my own hands.

I turn you to the sun
and hold you there,
waiting to see
what will open in the light.

The Fourth Lie

You say: I dreamt, and not: I lied.
When you wake up, it's a strange bed.
You open the door, shamefaced,
on a room so devastated

you run for the lift to the ground floor.
It tings, says, 'Doors closing.'
There are lies flying in the air
utterly grey from living upside down.

TENDER TAXES

The Sleeper

Let me go back to sleep, please;
you promised every time we fought.
Now I watch for moonrise
to switch off my heart.

Death. Sweetness. Words
wind up feeling – high, low,
veins, arteries, sappy stuff – hazards
I rush at until my own fear isn't fear.

You make me call you Lord Sleep,
force me to beg and laugh, cry and dream,
anything to stop the internal Eve
peeling out of my flank with her scary love.

Pegasus

Every girl's loved a horse once, as fiery as Pegasus,
his gallop, his breathy run, even the full stop
hers. Mine punctuated the air with hooves, crushed
the earth underneath until it exploded into water.

I was always waiting for Pegasus, ready to dabble
fingers in the sparks which gushed from his hoof-prints.
Can you feel how the sweetness tries to master you?
How your neck is learning to be curbed by flowers?

The Nativity Story

What could three Magi
bring to the party?
A little bird in a cage,
an enormous key

from a far-off realm
and the balm
my mother used to buy
made from strange lavender

which grows only round here.
You mustn't speak ill of these shreds.
They were enough to turn my child
into God.

To a Friend

They've peeled open this Madonna's heart,
exposed it to sun and dirt,
shoved in five sword-tips for sport.
They've peeled open her heart.

Yours is better sheltered, I hope,
and though grief thinks you're just its type,
her heart is the real dreamscape.

Her body isn't flesh any more;
your heart sits under your ribs, so close,
this close, to sheer exposure
but it's never flowered like her rose.

'L'Indifferent'
(*Watteau*)

I wish I were more like him:
ardent, sad, brought here
to be the witness – tender
as he is in his daft clothes –

to multiple surprises
which don't involve him at all
and, still dressed in words, to smile
from far away at an elegant girl.

Prayer of One Not Indifferent Enough

My heart's the size of a big clenched fist,
a hard, squeezing muscle
in the centre, not the left of my chest,
its one job, moving this drizzle

of blood round the body, a hassle
some days so worthwhile
I wish the tender right ventricle
– like the moon, my tears – would just fail.

Dinner with Rilke

Stay stock still if suddenly the angel
at your table decides to love you.
Pretend not to look by smoothing out wrinkles
in the cloth under the bread and ham.

Offer him your own food
casually, to taste in turn, so you
can watch beauty as he puts
an everyday glass to his lips.

You can't help yourself, though
he's avid for everything, eating,
kissing, anything to become you,
to repossess your house.

Prelude to Rilke

I stole his fingernail, still have it, blithe
enough watching it pick harp strings,
happy to hear his melodies against
the lullabies I hum under my breath
along with all those goodbye songs.

Song

Which of the organs inside
vibrates when angels sing?
Somewhere between
my kidneys and small intestine

a voice, tender and intrepid,
is humming tonight:
a bubble of wind, memory,
all my invisible mortality.

Night Work

Little lamp, I confide everything to your gooseneck,
pivot your face towards me, marvel
at your high-performance parabolic reflector.
You're all light, not heat, and you'll never tell.

Just like my old student lamp,
you want this reader, from time to time
to stop, astonished, looking at you,
until the other world goes monochrome.

(and your simplicity put an end to my angel)

Ink

Lovers and writers are the devil
for finding words which rub out:
the spot on the page
has no memory.

They insist on invisible perseverance
while telling the world
there's not the slightest track
of our steps, not one mark.

The Walk

I'm worrying, when I fret at night,
will I have told it all before I split:
how awe became ordinary,
and intercession. Rilke

and me, a summer day on the common,
mad for each other, drunk on scent –
any blossom – mad for words, breathing in
the pure perfume of our identity.

And now he's over there, going:
how can I make him pass for an image?
His shirt-tail floats more alive than this line
which falls in love with him all over again.

In a Park

Towards the end of that path
a stone's laughing, the one
with my littlest underneath.
I'll sing her this song:

should satellites, doves,
magpies, airships fly over
I'd strip off their shadows
to cover your grave.

The Fifth Lie

Telling lies seems easy for you, Angel:
you're the road even when stood still.
So lend me a hand here, be a pal
while we hunt down together what was real.

Hunter or hunted, remember this first:
she, the one surfacing, will be different
(too much music hurts my skin),
different from the man who dived in.